The Lewknor Turn

Anthony Mellors

*The
Lewknor
Turn*

Shearsman Books

First published in the United Kingdom in 2013 by
Shearsman Books
50 Westons Hill Drive
Emersons Green
BRISTOL
BS16 7DF

Shearsman Books Ltd Registered Office
30–31 St. James Place, Mangotsfield, Bristol BS16 9JB
(this address not for correspondence)

www.shearsman.com

ISBN 978-1-84861-308-9

ACKNOWLEDGEMENTS
Some of these poems have appeared in *Great Works, Poetry Wales, Angel
Exhaust* and *Paper and Ink*. An earlier version of 'The Gordon Brown
Sonnets' was published by Verisimilitude, and excerpts from 'bent out of
shape' are featured in Penny Hallas' multimedia *Orpheus* project.
My thanks to Penny, and also to Zoe Barratt, Kelvin Corcoran,
Lyndon Davies, Andrew Duncan, Allen Fisher, Peter Philpott,
David Rees, Zoë Skoulding, and Simon Smith.

Contents

bent

out

of

shape

He was afraid to stop his engine, declaring it was a devil to start again, but he would steer in circles until I got back. So I dived in and made for the cave which yawned like the lopsided upper jaw of a whale (the lower jaw being submerged, about thirty feet above the sea). As I swam inside a number of swallows flew out and I could see their little nests clinging to the cave walls and the flanks of stalactites. The cave grew much darker as it penetrated the mountain-side, and a couple of bats, which must have been hanging from the roof, wheeled squeaking towards the light. The roof sank lower, and, swimming along the clammy walls, I found a turning to the right and followed it a little way in; but it soon came to a stop. I tried all the way round and swam under water to see if there was a submerged entrance to another sea cave beyond. But there was nothing. The ceiling had closed in to about a foot and a half overhead, as I could now touch it with my hand. The air was dark but under the surface the water gleamed a magical luminous blue and it was possible to stir up shining beacons of phosphorescent bubbles with a single stroke or a kick. Strangely, it was not at all sinister, but, apart from the coldness of the water which the sun never reaches, silent and calm and beautiful. The submarine light from the distant cave-mouth makes an intruder seem, when he plunges phosphorous-plumed into the cold depths, to be swimming into the heart of a colossal sapphire.

Reaching Psamathus, where the quails are so thick in the air it is said you cannot separate the earth from the stars for them, I could see a black cavemouth across the bay from a wonky skeleton beacon, its lower jaw submerged and appearing to suck in vast quantities of the grey, choppy water as if it were dedicated to creating a restless microclimate within the turquoise calm of the peninsular. The sky was cloudless, the air dustily hot, yet the sea here looked more Atlantic than Aegean as it hustled the yachts moored in front of a glum row of battened tavernas and the mini-market. I scampered up to the promontory to get a better look at the cave, past the newly whitewashed church of Agios Nikolaos, behind which lay piles of discarded picture frames and bleached and paint-spattered prints of icons, and hopped my way along the finger of dazzling white rocks until I reached the iron skeleton. Convinced that I was looking across to the Entrance to Hades, I plotted how I could get closer without drowning in the turbulent water or falling from the vertical face above the cave. But a moment's reappraisal of the maps and books made me realize I was looking at everything the wrong way round and that the actual, modest and de-mythologized entrance lay where I had already been, at the mouth of one of the little inlets below the ancient spolia known as the Temple of Poseidon. The real cave could be seen only by swimming between moored caiques into a tiny cove where the sea was transparent, calm, and unhurried; it was roofless, well above the waterline, with no trace of a tunnel leading into the underworld (as Pausanias found), and guarded by nothing more menacing than a shrub that looked like hemp and an odalisque on a brightly-coloured beach towel. This was it, this wasn't it. I was entranced.

I

Intensively self-mythologized over the years
though an archaic element could not be shaped
he wormed his way into grim confidence
with none of the achieved serenity of the Sun-god Apollo.
In a kind of alchemical storm, all life escapes
as a viscous secretion, fetid smoke, and boiling refuse
wispy hair blown by clouds
the word *affectionate* carefully crossed out
eroded by exchange in the wet mouths of users
as in this thicket, *selva oscura*
invisible spheres formed in fright of contact in dreams
with the father-image both ghost and corpse
through the dockland and the wide streets of the modern city
there on the uplands going down to the marsh
a love for slowly moving things
a desire to feel the movement of time
of the singular though not unique advent into existence
the place without place of an intimate gaping
or gawping as if time itself could be fixed
sensing the blood flow inside as if watching a stream
the lines like ploughing a field, definitive break with song
fragments in the vernacular *figura morta*
'cruel as the tigers of Ircania' though a kind of lived substance
may emerge for the subject in such access of mind.

II

Complete time has singularity built in
or so the shroud of rag comforts those who quail
born of starstroke darkly haloed
by their interlocking shadows
glowing red and green through the fabric of a tent.
Terebinth which has for its coloured object
only the contoured surface
of blooming flesh-pink salves
desert macerations and the unity of consciousness
subject to change in a region of eternal truths
blessed by Hermes drinking lemonade and zibib.
Love-tokens kept as sentimental relics work
a lovely little situation
frescoed prelates on the wall of a narthex
cling grimly to an echo of this same love of self
notwithstanding fire of thorns
acoustic eros a philosophy softened with fables
most spiritual among bodies indefinable
the colour of white bones or bared nerves.
Vast logs burn slowly all through Advent
a fresh leak of pain on the spiritual shelf
the high point of the ritual rare
scattered and fugitive like natural beauty
except that no part of nature is beautiful.

III

Pasiphae, pacify our ecstacy and revolt
as high winds snap the washing-line
and rectangles of bright light fade the sofa
under the window and the patina
on the shaft of a crook turns pale green.
It is an easy and automatic defection
to wash smoke and rust off the ikons:
we don't suck out of dry rivers these days
in the textual suburbs though following
may lead us by noise in the streets
to a city transformed into sea
possible neumes and flexions
where there are no trees for the cicadas.
Corporate imaging softens and deepens
a plastic technique in saffron and mauve
pretending not to know what human means
though it may have no use for it
or have a use for it but the wrong one
fumbling for change as if all that matters
is the coinage of needs unaware
of the real existence led by women
shining wide in a portable wooden cow.
Mooching in shops for remission of debt
entranced by a snow-white form.

IV

What pleases us is the adaptation
of the object's form to our faculties
this body that hoped to flower and become
a flute in the frost, violet in a crucible
compelled to feel the distances
when a cold rain falls outside the hut
as if drawing down the virtues of the upper world
by tweaking the lower ones
sunburnt shales and grassless crags
not as we live in everyday banality
but born into an enchanted world
reading dense and mistaken texts
charged by deep country silence
except for odd rustlings in the laurel-heart
fantasms that cannot bear the revelation of speech
as a lower limit or mist of some sort
garb to be abandoned in law or end
the plenitude of form which kills form
making appearance dissolve itself
while still remaining appearance
dazed as they move toward the slaughter house
for there never was a void to be filled
or a view to the depths of the earth
every thing lucid to every other.

V

An art of conversation and bleared eyes
yet vines still grow over the fallen walls
and shadows of birds cross the brickwork
taken up into the text of a lost epic, recovered at last
like a phase opposition or drag in the system
incapable of becoming an element of cognition
the cinders some forest spirit saw fit
chalk the turf's secret igniting against grey
chromatic units without system
only in the shades grow cords of yellow cedar bark
like laurels / divine fingers stretched towards
some explicit link that never comes
and cannot choose between the handy-dandy of opposites.
Summer as an image of chaos, persistence of the trope
text with no shadow or fertility where lichen eats the vigour of
        the stalk
arrives at violence of opinion merely
tramping through our allotment in heavy boots
Apollo the lizard-slayer an alarming sight at dawn
when the early light makes a *grisaille* of the interior
recalled in dreams: barrows, labyrinths
cold stares at the windings of pathways
a vacant and superior surface
where you are enjoined to take your seat by the stove:
few things happen at the right time and the rest do not happen
        at all.

VI

They drop in at every cafeteria
in towns sick of rebel subjects and tyrant masters
fit for nothing but to be cut into shadows
each pain falsified by guilt, wretched
under dark ilex / narcissus bloom on alders
marking a cross with lamp-black on the lintel
partial to the dark-brown pumice of twice-baked bread
salves and rustic epithalamia
lenten potlatch when the wind is southerly
the growing threat within us of desire and demand
a waste that allows us to recognize order
charms against bad crops or intercourse with the devil
pouncing upon the young like carrion crows
eager as glow-worms blinking up at eventide.
The resort to a logic of contamination
natural property of human labour / surplus
thick with dried stalks and withered sedge
when we do not know what to do for hunger and nakedness
going in and out to find pasture
not the first mortals to see beauty in the beautiful
preserve old discord denied by woodwork
and swollen obtuse stems / interval
between image and concept ruffled with goods:
stenachoria in a fire of thorns.

VII

They still smoke Peter Stuyvesant round here
and white dog shit can be found
dry on the roadside by reeking bins
or lurking in gritty crevices
like the shadows made by rayguns.
What was a sharp scent in the mountains
is down here in Pephnos night-thick:
sage, thyme, jasmine, a library of once damp
now dried books, and the hot whiff of bedpiss.
In the morning, sweet hot figs collapsed on walls
and snapped plastic pegs litter the way
by an eroded limestone beach / flower of the visible
a sudden consistency between incompatibles
as the sun seizes you by the hair
on a terraced path of steps
lined with asphodel and stinking inula.
Little dogs honk like geese in a distant grove
and the day thickens into dream
wheeled squeaking towards the light
up to Thalamai where they say there is a spring
and bronze statues of Pasiphae and Helios
less of a sanctuary than the faded deckchair
two pints of iced water and sesame bar needed
when hands are fat and unclenchable from the heat.

VIII

Also the ants here have a whiter colour
than is usual especially on the little isle
where foot-high statues of the Dioskouroi once stood.
Their non-being alone is their *qualitas occulta*
though for the helmsman in his rubber dinghy
rays from heaps of earth studding the shoreline
reach an accord with language itself
understood as a lack of order
or tangible analogue of silence interrupted
by cups of coffee handed through smokeswirls
the occasional cigarette and repellant coils
had for two obols in the market at Stoupa.
This whole place is called Apia, 'of the pear-tree'
and at this end there is mere amazement
where fertility is concerned where wind-skewed
we went at the latemouth sovereign in elegy
a thousand described routes to the fruitful womb
but I shall not be pedantic enough to list them
yet all the while it would be true that the mind
oversimplifies its materials and few of us
are not in some way infirm
approaching the dump with a nasal stop
and warm negus, blooded and kept warm
buoyed every yard or so with a hollow gourd.

IX

'Saw here the ruin of old cloister and old ruins
arches and large high walls, walks, cold baths
and holy wells, the one with a stone to kneel upon
with the naked knee and after crossing himself with water
(which is all spring water and never freezes) and drinking
a glass of the water and wishing for any matter or thing
(as I said before on naked knee) such shall sure and happen.
The other well being of stone as well as the well and the troughs
is for dipping people for certain complaints
the whole well walled in and the fields planted to great extent
not kept up and the arches and buildings all falling down
except two very high arches or gate-ways and the house
which has been large and noble at present in decay
although it has been new-faced next the garden
and new-sashed within fifty or sixty years.'
Instead, a dull urban waste reveals itself:
no sensuous green mounds swell up like desire
though the leaky tap has stopped dripping
and my hair is the colour of dandelion fluff
especially when the sun slants across it
or as when Osiris blows it as in silly poems
dedicated to the well being of *rus in urbe* charlatans
always lifting up their hope in the hope that metaphor
will relieve them of the adequate symbol.

X

A sudden heat as the manure truck goes by
on those long miles beyond Newmarket
reconciles concept and intuition in another world
southwards to the heart of London
a defunct movement ready for asset-stripping
in what they call the cold light of day
but north is towards wilderness
where you point out diffusion, anchorage, and fixation
a daring little frill round the hem of normal discourse
the work of mourning without work
threnody in a wheelbarrow and church-darkened pond
carefully traced in the angle of a skeletal arm
somewhere behind the back of the brain
half sleeping not even stirring and the trees
to vent the overflowing of their heart
send branches verging waterwards over the field
partly like wings impressed on the eye
all bent out of shape from flood to world's end
as those canary-sucking bishops attest
the Church forgets what is meant to be reactionary
where beyond the extreme sea wall
we need not boggle at the word hypnosis
Quomodo sedet sola civitas
the perfect fox-proof roost for nightfall

XI

As the visitor leaves the factory gates
it seems that the streets and boulevards glow
centuries away from cuneiform writing
but time has failed to erase the written word
a wave and a shout from dim fields and long sad halls
resting in notches of this palisade / shade vanished
and then the quietus of sunlit uplands
offered as gift, hand, or logos, a halo
spilt into the folds and twists of a great ephemeral skin
waves folding back on themselves
built-in to the end-user
in the sense that a visual and temporal frame breaks
refusing to be passed-off as representation
and in a movement beyond subjectivity deliria
does not gloss over this split in the half-body
which dirty concrete work has rendered shonky
following round this circle in time and space
shadows in the cave of that sunlit world
never fails to invest regions as if it could *not*
lead us to all manner of games and festivals
an artificial caste manured with laurels
both genteel and common values of the polis
halo stripped from the state machine
even a bird's song has more freedom in it.

XII

Therefore in the field's unease and the darkened wood
come down like rain into a fleece of wool
the red glow of an *illy* sign marks off distance
between 'seasonable resort' and a hillbilly smackdown
among broken glasses and the ticking of the gramophone
which show we are only a footstep from the garden
in the finite sphere where we cannot get over difference
whatever it gives or takes or is hard of access
links afternoon haze with surveys from exile
lemons glowing like lamps on the borders of a dusty market
cow-punk leaking from unsheltered doorways
a place to deambulate for a couple of hours
spurred-on by coffee and the driest cream horn
an abuse finessed into a work of art
at least until the harrowing trek resumes in the free
slow fall of the evening / among smashed masonry
rusted olive tins scattered with glow-white ironstone
all the phantasmata of the pagan ones
baulked by flying sparks tindered in doldrums
as if it began from a single centre
opposed to its diffuson and fragmentation imperfect
time posited as superfluous time 'if read as hole'
like a rare book long out of print you might translate
were there a chance of it being had for a song.

XIII

The horn's open bell painted with faded nosegays
aural channels flooded with soma and what the hell
is the ragman calling through a megaphone?
For the price of an obol proprioception
with no middle-man fucking-up the works
an American counter-practice with no kind of tongue to it
these splintered fragments of living substance
leaning forward snapping a close-up of the face
immuno-compromised upcycling where not willing
is not a practicable state of mind
for I have lost someone very close to me
swollen-footed Oedipus that I am
finding joy in a bargain box of misshapes
ethical beginnings from a point of no-value
like the legendary Dulwich cobblers a waste of time
instruments in a spiritual exercise
displacement of themselves towards nature
the causal mythology of the 9/11 premodern
some sort of lost wax or other process
where the initial armature gets scrapped towards the end
and a history of ghosts which never return to the main line
stripped down to waking life in a series of episodes
controlled explosions in a quicksand of thought
of, of, of: the sentence that says nothing and does nothing.

XIV

Who *was* Frank Moore? Spent the day worrying
that I'd missed a bit, meaning the organized dance
of a non-thesis. The sign said use drywipe pens only
only the wipe wasn't dry and later a black nodule
the colour of the seat turned out to be solid waste
that wasn't solid and I was afraid. The final turn
is toward Lewknor, rainbows in the streetlamps
unfathomed for all their limpidity, readymade
icons of a journey to the centre of the hearth.
How two handfuls of meat produce all those
visual fireworks is like a joke after dinner
because you thought it would aid digestion, so
absolute utility equals absolute risk, but if you sniff
you can smell the incense, and other things less
appealing to private economic holdings, or the distortion
on another surface, of an image embedded
in the flow of a lifestyle. Nothing is more commercial
than alchemy, and the lumps stuck to the shirttails
stretch back through time to a place aliquid
the whole essence thus composed placed in act
broken but shuffling along regardless
where the final turn may be that valuelessness
is itself closed off by ideology. So what
motivates change? Forces attracted and repelled?

XV

In the case of the wheat token ritual has to be observed
on the customary stroll down the main street
scarce in being called the best of nature framed
being the concept of an inadequate object
the raisin cluster and cake of figs
fit garnish for the heart of a Smurf
with something tightly-packed inside
where the eye of spirit and the loving eye coincide
in dangerous assymetric threats
approaching the bottom corner through a scheduled gap
tight buds turned to the sun as if the tooled response
were not enough, not welcome in the house of no imagination
not unconform to other shining globes that lead you
through a small kissing-gate into a field
of flat, shaded planes, more transparent than opaque
the law standing still, as the sun does in solstice
as *solstitium* – an interval or suspension
and the track begins to bend round to the right
almost before you know it and the whole cadre /
cadaver of poets comes gimping along: one-handed
ruptured, dispraxic, related to the oneness of gathering
with a mysterious inner light some have called the blurring of
          the heart
which shows itself above all in marginal conditions:
if one has only one slit, one does not get any fringes.

XVI

All civil affairs stopped and mania suspended
the *schadenfreude* felt on finding the place
abandoned and derelict (no one goes in
and no one leaves) soon replaced by contempt
that it was to make way for a new housing estate
rebranded for some unknown reason as the deposits
of dead yeast. There's no restoration here—
they gave a pound for every body removed
in the 'thick' of winter / ice shagging the firs
and electric dust in the air after ECT jolts
forged permanent links between Wisteria and hysteria.
Then Syringa Ward, hymning Largactil
and its by-products, Aporia reincarnated
as a boy with a silver-topped cane and delusions
we all experience from time to time, though if I said
'literal', tell me about autonomy, tell me about
pictorial configurations of collapsed units,
frosted lampshades left on concrete sills and false
teeth scattered on rubber floors. Randomization
causes clumping, a state of exception no replacement
by gated community or convulsive laughter
will keep out. In spite of dome cams children
hang about the chronic block and play in echelon wards
where coming out alive makes you into someone else.

XVII

A final shot of the emergency indicator
and after turning a slight bend the collusion forcing
words into collision is oddly painful though this is only
to be expected given—and I say given in full knowledge
that the gift is impossible—a Vertov-like compendium
of sounds and field recordings in the teeth of Wisteria
my house not propped by Taenarian columns
or the rich flora of sustained reflection where
there is no shuffling in sleep, gold, shadows, gifts
all this, and no ammonia, and when summertime was over
I looked without seeing, listened without hearing
passing through a cottage once called Hunger Spot
but now Sunny Bank, a reflection of the peasant
paganism of that country in the second century
a finality in the realm of means the power of gesture
that interrupts the gesture, the camp being a space
that opens up a locale without order to find some way
over the marsh tracks to some place that would welcome
me, in sight but too far away to cause harm / to come
quietly on to the land and spread over it
this blackened warren hung with cobwebs and swags
of elderflower scenting the air with cat's piss
cloud-shadows moving across ramparts and eyes
some foolishness shaped by the vulgar hand.

XVIII

An owl was driving away bees from the entrance to a wine-cellar
where the body of sea-green lay who spat in the mouth of the one
whose name was already the name of what he'd become
at the margins of thought who holds to faith whenever rain begins
always disguised beneath other names at once voiced and voiceless
and out of and across the salt flood where the air grows cold
in a dark summer after frosts had done for the rosemary
but not for the knotweed which spired up under the fence
and had to be dug up and burned with the blackened sprigs of
          sea-dew
charging memory perhaps though with slower recall
bamboo's internal resonance mixed with echoing drips
those absences we call silence punched holes in the fabric of time
as if emerging from a mist as we once emerged each morning
O yes mon loup the heavy ox sets chest to briar and branch
adds random background noise to simulate the crack and plop
moths make as they twist inside a paper lamp
the mapping of chaotic fluctuating conditions possible
skipping damaged areas / halo and burr to the force of image
not to overflow the present but to have distance
as to a being to come and the impossibility of retreat
from the lives we're living and what we're doing – no oxygen
in that world where you can be organic and pagan and still
use microbeats and a lot of whispery vocals to make
loop films of semi-naked people engaged in pointless tasks.

XIX

I like those Italian goat-films
with early glimpses of shepherd life.
Perplexed by miracles and dust-devils
they stay out all spring and summer
searching in the sun for another overload
and watch the boundaries during winter
helpless in the face of those already in power
reduced to gyrating prawns
willing to work but unwilling to find it
the old woman's infinite humanity
bores everyone shitless
with hilarious consequences
since fuck it, they're not hardwired into anything
industriously tunneled by insects
nor self-regulating networks
swollen with tribute and two forms of expression
silence and rage in a desolate canyon
ashen helves the pallor of a bone-yard.
In the limiting case –reproduction ratio
(the killing of animals for management purposes)
total displacement has a normal distribution
equal to blanket ring culls
bodies sprayed with napalm and torched
will not wake again in this world.

XX

The Thornbush Cock Giant insists
everyone live in permanent disorder
tie little black dogs to the radiator
arrange single dead moths on window-sills
love men who think marital means martial
in a land where anything can happen
with heavy equipment and a virus
running in the background
the sudden mustard-flare of charlock
common in artificial communities
where peasants are slow to cast clouts
and masculine hysteria is almost unknown
an astonishing world of velvet jackets
paisley ties bistros and high-class scrubbers
recalled balls in Fiume
magical when you can feel anything
the exception being the Homeric corpus
in contrast with the principle of free speech
green-lit and funded by the very outlet
that gave history its 'greatest hits'
like a series of appalling farts
anchored by the Latin term *fascinum*
a timelag of several hundred milliseconds
before death, life, joy, song.

XXI

Felt a shade better yesterday
it was not one of those days when you
wind up as a pathetic sideshow clown
earwigs in the loaf and gas
released by inwardly rotting vegetables
I cannot live without you and so on
in unending manifold varieties
sprayed across the rood screen
of your worshipful and desecrated self
but somehow lighter
betrothed among well-wishers and spies
a meticulous and increasingly cruel
figurative but ambiguous space
'the outward shining of a lambent flame within'
ha ha magical when you feel anything
more than the nervous jerks of the Creeleyesque
impossible as a British road movie
the little car chugging round public sphericules
and blocks of unaffordable affordable housing
a stranger to yourself firmly guided
by essentialist thought
changing spatial expressions
patterns of inclusion and exclusion
from which I flow away.

XXII

Since all negative persistence is damaging
this darkness suits you well
even in midsummer when heat will not come
though windows are left open
and there is no fire in the hearth.
They say the night has a thousand eyes
black eyes cut through to skulls
yet distance determines intensity
for the endless denial of limits
blind to one's own blindness
and my *gageure* split into faggots
discharged by means of flexible rods
to kindle the thought of Greek parallels
where none exist – another enduring relic
up in smoke, substance of the living order
viewed through a mugwort wreath
a puppet dragged to the bleaching heath
or carted about the village on off days
with burlesque pomp the bastards
expecting dole of half-boiled peas
from the optician Coppola
as if to rattle the foreign body within ourselves
like a doll hidden beneath a shroud
ferment silent and sublime.

XXIII

We may expect a special core of feeling present
in open spaces and forward units
where remote intimacy takes place
almost as if there should be no story
peering through the gloom towards this fragile craft
for one awful moment immersed
in mother's arms the blue wool bed-jacket
and a heavy swell in the Broad
pushed up the aisle in an old bath chair then
from the lodge gates down to the water's edge
bits of straw flying across the air
watching the line of thatch against a raging sky
could hear them shout to each other
as the elms sighed and creaked that old stump
met by two policemen in a boat
pushed far enough to get to the opposite
of what you're saying
at the back of the Red Cross cupboard
bad faith leads to bad blood
so easy to get simple folk to kill
in the right circs such as general unrest
faces streaked with tears assymetric
kinetic threats me hearties figures
moving backwards and forwards along the spit.

XXIV (aside)

Pause you who read this
and think of the long chain of iron or gold
fast moving consumer goods
renewed day after day for eternity
the mysterious nature of human choice
(liver and onions—does that grab you?
a Lucullan feast by Athonite standards)
lights moving about in the upper windows
now littered with sherds
too complex to have arisen
from mechanical causes alone
a gyro-movement in the tripod head
that 'turns' when it turns
in the short-run to bejewelled weapons
the austere symbols of extra-terrestrial
majesty and cool shaded ways
in the long-run to crumbling diazomas
stone reliefs of puny figures
a dirt road to the south
and slender funerary vessels
with a black base and neck
dark doe-like eyes and crimson stucco
conceived in purely military terms
as the blankness of a monolith.

Homage
to
Rod
McKuen

No reserve
no reserve left
of a love without reserve.
How could there be a lover tomorrow
or any other day
if there's nothing left?
My disingenuousness
speaks tomes.

Where have the curlews gone?
the estuaries and the moors are bare
of them, and no warmer climes
claim them.

Sitting in the mouth of my cave
I watch 'ladies' trapped by the tide
and think of simple things
like panting hounds, attractive clams
and the night's curfew.

It's impossible to see
the sun go down
or the moon come up
without losing sight
of all that you love

for eyes are enough
to sense the rankness
of another man's breath
on your face.

As Morrissey says
you have never been in love
until you've seen the dawn rise
behind the home for the blind.

It's true, it's all
sodding
true.

The love you didn't give me
is all the love I've known

hard to understand
in the light of my radiance

captured on the tube
in crooning paroxysms

but there you go
it's not what you've had

but what you do with the notion
that starbursts in the mind

that false memories
take the place of the so-called real

flowers bloom like winter Echina
poppies appear in the snow

and I know you I know you
as if something had never not yet happened.

I don't know what it means
for days to keep secrets
only that secrets are what I live
day in and day out

since I became strung out
on your stringing me along

and the days I have left
eked-out in swallowed desire.

The curling sandwich
of my misplaced love for you

remains on the plate
remains on the dresser
adored for its age and worms

its hidden drawers filled with twine
coltsfoot, stubs of charcoal,
light fittings that didn't fit:
the pointless array of disarray.

Dogs eat all kinds of things.
Like me, they're not fussed
except when I opened the can
of premium meaty chunks
you bought last Tuesday
and they turned up their noses
choosing to snuffle in the briar-patch
and lick at their own turds
as if puzzled by their appearance.

Tell me you still smile
that the howls of arctic wolves
remind you of nights before the fire
when we tracked each other's scent
unafraid of the territory.

I can't trust myself
to do good always
foaming at the mouth
with need for you

King Priam faced
the nature of choice
saw the sun set
but drank wine with Achilles

if you would just leave
if I could leave
there would still be mornings
red skies, hanging vines

That old bear
I've kept since childhood
has lost its growler

you press his belly
repeatedly
(hands like mittens)

but no sound will come
remember this
when I hold my tongue

There's a word for what I do
kitsch
I can't help it
if it means no robins
the scent of woodsmoke
on crisp Sonoma mornings
picnics and redwoods
footprints washed away by tides
left there for aeons
to be washed into view again
like a love that disappears
only to become strangely new
I can live with that
though you don't have to.

Most girls have boyfriends
assigned them at birth.
If a man didn't intervene
now and then
he'd always be lonesome.
Lonesome and free
but it's not like freedom
when I'm left still as a lizard
basking on the mesa
as you go back to the one
or other who will always be there
calming the infants
straightening lawns
making everything right when
all I can do is wrong.

To those who go on
spending their summers in Nice
overwintering in Gstaad
to whom the clink and fizz
of drinks on the terrace
makes the day begin and end
all I can say is think of me
reclining on a bed of nails
of my own making
like the last fakir in a land
where the trees drip rain
and the suburbs escape into fog.

They tell me rabbit
fancying's on the wane.
Just my luck to be
coming in to something
when it's on the way out.
Was getting proper
into it and all but now
will have to man-up
and accept it for what it is:
my sublimation of the loss
of you, your flowering
footfall attendant
on my place of birth your
curling fingers no lucky
charms or keepsakes
adhesive
              maternal wrapping
the pause before you speak.

Let the partridges cackle
my little deer, and leave
the frogspawn bubbling
in the pond to remind us
that we come from this
and that all the energy I mustered
learning to know you
had its force stopped by brambles
when all I wanted was to make
a clearing, by the old mill
instead of civilized silence
the thickets into which we roam
with a view back to suburban
lairs
      mock-tudor gables
and gnomes dotting the lawns
like the dry husks of men in Pound's
seventh canto.
          Like me.

I'm as blind as a fag
who knows a door is open
only when the wind's banging it.
Who lives like a house without windows
and leans awkwardly on his crutch.
I know only the wind in the street
and its tumbleweed connection.
The crutch you are to me
and the strange sounds at night
in boarded tenements.

Months have passed since you came to me
and I learned joy in your petals
the tragic splash of flowering Judas
                              your smile

smiles of a summer night.

I pride myself that there were many others
before you, tokens of my self-regard.

How could it be otherwise?

Even when pissed as a fart
Nicolas Cage scores
according to the movies
and I'm not about to let go the zeitgeist
which equates lonely with the abuse
you inflict on others.

So I watched patterns on the ceiling
from this bed or that bed
biding my time, passive as the truly phallic
who do not have to try
assured that one day you would arrive
to take from me the pressure of ennui
light as a bird
your legs like tall grasses shimmering
before the wind from the sun.

Thighs don't speak, though we pretend they do
nor the heart
which might as well be in the knee
          third leg from the sun
                    sky crooked and every which way

emblems of the love I share
or think I share
not knowing where you will be tomorrow
in some downtown bar
scooped-up by some deadbeat lothario
          (the way I could never be)
while I maintain my exile
cooing over dogs and Christmas cards
my absent family rosy in firelight
and a station-wagon purring in the yard.

Epigrams

Crisp though the sonic grid might seem
beyond five decades of word salad
rubbish mistranslates as radish.
He that speaks in an unknown tongue
edifies himself, spirit joined with voice
without the mediation of meaning.

The vel of alienation as a serving suggestion:
sooner or later, everything turns against itself,
coolness has meaning only by being not uncool.

A sense of self-satisfaction
pervades the market in narrow competencies.
Hard-wired in the Pleistocene to hunt and gather
the family invests in sentiment, a black talent
for snap-action coupling and transit lounge
handshakes. Rain is always driving in
from the West to the Land of Sores.
Is the room light and airy?

The room is airy but not light.

That tea-shop you liked with the watercress buns
has ceased trading. The rain stopped briefly
and we enjoyed the ride home in fine weather,
though we all felt an odd separateness
when we passed the new sex shop at Guyhirn.

Impossible object at the beginning of time
where the voice originates like a pitch invasion
in outer darkness. A singularity is when nature
breaks down and we don't know what to do.

Another motif is that of the 'single survivor':
full of profit but off your squiff
once you get inside their houses
people stop being people.
These stereotypes occur wherever
potatoes are grown.
All a poet can do today is annoy.

the quality is the beauty
the subject is the house
nor is the distinction chimerical
the music of birds or fall of waters
mere figure or appearance
foreign and external objects connected
with trifles bear the father's name
a double relation of impression and idea
remarkable for its novelty
powerful motives of interest and danger
the port and gait of a swan or turkey
elevated with joy
to communicate with daemons drops down
sunk in the new relation.

on earthly branch
under black stele
up gentle ruth

my wretched state
the first to leave
this weary night

tossed brain
fed with words
note shrill

Song echt

So if
it was

made plain
to her

song echt
no brain

could you
place it?

Try the
black prairies

that surround
Ely or

the vast
coastal nothingness

at Gedney
Drove End—

this is
flatness to

the point
of obscuring

the coastal
shelf.

Perhaps soon
we'll all

live as
the fenlanders

used to
punting through

sedge between
islands of

quiet habitation.

The Gordon Brown Sonnets

for Andrew Lawson
Spring 2009

Maundy is doled where lenten justice shines;
you go for gold, the spud you like.

And therefore also they judge of human actions by the event; for
being uncapable of operable circumstances, or rightly to judge the
prudentiality of affairs, they only gaze upon the visible success,
and therefore condemn or cry up the whole progression.
   —Sir Thomas Browne, *Pseudoxia Epidemica, or Enquiries*
into very many Received Tenents and commonly Presumed Truths.

I

In the softening gloom of mid-November
fill the bin with gold, with unwearied
finger, a brisk canon by the terrace
sung from the root. Let minister invent
the feeble sonnet of supine content
from a mound of rubbish, now embarrass
the ones he failed to address, period.
On the clifftop a rosy welfare screed
reported cheek, unsatisfactory
the humble vetch belied instanter
to its unfolded bloom, the martial weed
rejected then. I can't begin to tell
how the rot set in, sufficient to say
the glottal stop had ceased to signify.

II

Sufficiency of ritual, the hum
of mighty workings in a distant mart,
easy for simple men to understand
but not those parasitic *rentiers*
voices mingled with the sigh of spring wind,
their faith erect through interior gloom
and wholesale selloff of the terror stakes.
The question is whether to stick or twist
as you are driven away like a beast
into a lonely spot in the forest
or on the marshes, the clods stark and dry
underfoot. And that low voice of second
existential zeal. Or ring of glory
charged with reason, ten seconds to munter.

III

That low voice again, fed into the stream
like a Farley's rusk submerged in milk
at last subsumed into the new Brit empire.
Mourning cards hang in ranks, their sable
borders offset by the cool, creamy walls
and huge compressors of ammonia
visible from the sash, all that remains
of the Fray Bentos meat-processing plant.
The stream runs close to its empty carcass
varnishing the struts of an enthymeme
rotisserie: who waits in silence here
enjoys the minister's pater noster,
the hope that all who delve and spin beneath
his honest palm will do their level best.

IV

Nothing but a huge and abandoned plant,
a quick trip from the Argentine Blackpool,
its grey abattoirs and storage houses,
cranes and wharves, are a national monument.
Wheels, pipes, lamps and cables, a uniform
pale brown, have frosted into a cast-
iron cobweb, a battery of dials,
red levers and switches rusted into
a perpetual off. Sturdy chairs are hitched
to solid wooden desks, each one laid out
with a new twist on the full battery
of middle management. A shrublike stand
for rubber stamps. An in-tray, an out-tray,
gleaming brass rails in the cashier's office.

V

My foot descends, shrunk with gainful pleasure
at the peasant's grave, or roaming hand, long
past the fix time of deciduous man
which girds the streaming crape where Brown
has laced his terror-pact with grim resolve.
Now strangled fauces pinch the rancid brink
of this foul creek, the glowing lilac tuft
sings with monitory bell among the bents
from bearded ear to clod's hostile shelter.
Poor in heat the bleak verge soothes your fuddled
eyes, wet on the low embankment. Sloven
hands penetrate beneath a filmy skirt,
in swealing forks the huddled mits inclined
to workshy grip, raked tilth of mastic woe.

VI

'Gervase Babington in 1604 suggested that the Jubilee principle of distribution should be applied in time of plague and death, etc.' Christopher Hill, *The English Bible and the Seventeenth Century Revolution* (London: Penguin, 1994), 164.

Grey puppets jiggle in this hinterland:
I hear a beggar's kit scrape to the view
and my dear one binds the little mammets'
feet and hands in the fading winter light.

The weary Smith stands reeking, lucre
fake in a tartan wig, while those about him
nod their heads to the infant jubilee.

There, festive auto-tension incised
in lava-glaze and the half-forgotten
fired must of a Scheurich vase
will never blend into the beggar's frieze.

Where wings take dream, the cosy families
collapse, reform, then muddle on
like the void pledge on a failing unit.

VII

It is a world of interiors, blessed,
nostalgic for the heart of the country.
Those who run across the sea change their sky
but not their minds. Keen to chew scratchings
down in the galley they long to return
to the tame and blank lands from which they came,
striding out with outlaws clad in thick cloaks
at the summer solstice, hoicking thin drawers
in snowy weather, small and unconcerned
by the dark absence present at their backs.
Flummery it may be, but the concept
'delivers change within secure limits':
Some move it slow when the lictor dictates,
others quicken to the point of grebo.

VIII

A state of dereliction, graced with mould,
stove pipework riddled with holes: nothing
under the sun can be so fungible.
Here the crowned heads of Europe were taken
to sample fruit and veg and then returned,
keen for a good time with their ministers.
Flowers stand out on a blue-grey background
daubed with acacias, chestnuts and creepers.
Each panel bears a fruit tree at its core:
apple, peach, plum, cherry and apricot.
At human height *Viburnum opulus*,
begonias, nigella intertwine.
The rustic style was at its peak and led
oddly to a glut of strident beauty.

IX

Best not to balk or create despair
since provincial control is powerless
to check the carbon cycle feedback
and the graded objects *entfremdet*
at the heart of me entertain the law
no matter how much you curse, explode
or groan, tremble with dissatisfaction
and reaffirm the shelves in joyful plaint.
That old fogey who shoved me on the train
comes back at night to a 'period home
near-doubled in width', his offprint
of *Data Shadow* by Tony Lopez
aslant and bookmarked on the sofa,
fully aware that the message is bleak.

X

In a town roughly the size of Cambridge
desert winds carry the wind of stasis.
I praise your professionalism, courage,
and your patriotism—all the p's
and a c. For Hegel, the orators
are most clear when they speak the already known
by rote. The manner of subsistence is
chaos as vatic order, drifting on
a reed, *stridenti*, hard-wired to DNA
on multiple platforms. A new cohort
hustled into position. Facing the
spirit, others, appearances, seeing
red everywhere, strangely proud of endless
change we can believe in, bollocks du jour.

XI

Riding by on a sit-up-and-beg
you view a scuffle on surplus land.
The best false sense you can lay your hands on
slides away in a fur of Brownian noise.
For now, the ruckus is over; knowing
that fear rules the rulers too, you whizz on
caught in endless refraction, the effect
of plenitude, content and vertigo.
Eyes here, signs of the moneychanger
where all you can see is the goods made good
in a war on error. The 'exception',
meaning a state of emergency,
codes into daily life like a promise
on a banana box or orange crate.

XII

The crate brimming with produce: yellow fruit
copper green, fascination, blackblue ash
glory, corrupted stars, heavenly husk,
the Lord himself is he that was the foe.
Step away from the pie, there's no burrow
free from venture or radical error,
neither can you borrow your way out of
trouble, powered by permanent outrage
or the primed sense of self-satisfaction
held out against the bright obviousness
of mission creep. Lone star, the ash stranger
flickers in the dusk – now left to wander
in the carbolic light. Broke, frosted, may-
be give the vegetables a miss tonight.

XIII

In this wide world his wind heard, yet his form
not seen, plum in mouth, and tongue aside
crossing wet lips. Still, it tastes good to him
and in delayed premature blooming strays
in the meadow of its saying. Can we
account for ourselves though cowed and dogeared
buried in this dream of tired travellers
who keep going because they must, if at
lower pitch of inward feeling? Noah
sailed over the deepest flood that could be
or have been. Who on this earth ignorant
does not wonder at the motion of clouds
and the captive songs that long for freedom?
Focus on the past-perfect tense of 'bure'.

XIV

When all said and done it is a mild yoke:
you try to zero balance but always
holidays intervene like a cartload
of basic slag into the pattern of days
as it were strung out one to another
meant as a discrete series yet somehow
clogged and final. Hidden herbal powers
fret the tear ducts, the use you make of them,
mnemonic love crunch or chronic lenten
shuffle. Nick Drake sells cough drops *post mortem,*
Black Shuck plodding behind a Listerine
catafalque. Sorry to hear you lost out
in the race to the bottom. Still, console
yourself going forward riding westward.

XV

We now come to another aspect of
the imperial bent, monopoly,
its tendency to stagnate and decay.
This is due to retarding technical
progress. Someone would always have to stop
Alec Guinness from sporting a white suit
that never attracts dirt, scum comprising
an essential component of the growth
of a class which lives by clipping coupons.
Such parasitic and, frankly, mulish
behaviour secures the income of the
usurers, of whom Pound said hath no man
a home, not in the long run anyway,
though some of them contrive to all the same.

XVI
for B.M., in memoriam—no better late than never

We condemn the violence and must never
let it happen again, cowheels stuck up
in fired air, tripe screed spin-out across
husbandry channels, big new ideas
to help you break down silos. Head intact,
the feet drown in a sea of corruption
weeping sometimes, mistaken for laughter.
Tirelessly dragged feet, splayed on average
but driven to protect turf, peculiar
the odour from large shining colourless
laminae. Caught often from raw farm-fresh
meat leaving no taste in the mouth. Copy
voice or 'persona' must look as if it's coming
from the same company, no names win-win.

XVII

From moment to moment, just as it speaks,
the glistening self that guarantees the world
confronts at its heart that other absence
which is the condition of its being,
fly on the bank. Emotion lies within
the family and not outside. Friendship
remains secondary, celibacy a kind
of death. Even the liberation of
desire in schizo-revolutionary
nonsense bespeaks this rotten cordial fruit.
Watch what you say, avoid odd questions,
don't be seduced by anyone who gives
you shelter, approach with caution: worthless
patrons bring only trifles and torments.

XVIII

In this age of damp and uncertainty
there can be no return to the old days
the vacuous patois and random walk
and teeth cut on the confidence racket
nor predilection to laral nightmare
turning under yellow viscose sheets
as a lamp in the street flickers at dusk.
The patterned response is always too late,
a colonic wipe-out fuelled on white baps
deemed inconvenient but in theory
no risk to public health. Seen in relief
the tightly crammed stalls look hard as iron
yet their warmth and brightly coloured paper
bring solace and the freedom to commune.

XIX

Not that we should counter this in bad faith,
something suspended, even trapped in time,
darkness with twinkling lights, peep-box vistas
flush with mud like the crown of horny rays
the sun makes behind a cloud. Northern land
such as this cannot ripen southern fruit
and a hacienda in Ovingdean
will not change that. But we needn't follow
the warp of the sphere; floating out across
the vacant sod we meet the holy light
besprent when shadows fall on dewy grass.
In which, like the glory and the spectre,
each person creates their own maestum
released at last from cataracts and fog.

XX

Can we be sure that heavy plant is crossing?
Read the signs: they might look like us but they're
aliens all right, disfigured by fat
and alcohol, protected by the law,
subsisting on desire and toil. The one
who shouldered me in Argos must have been
in the torment of the spirit, struggling
but failing to rise to a higher state.
The all-seeing eye registered nothing
but a spunky handkerchief dropped no doubt
in the rush before closing-time. There must
be a link here between these monkey firms
and white terror, though official bodies
inquired and found no trace. Happy now?

XXI

Bring me your white metal, the reflection
of spirit back on itself—I'll turn it
to silver. Still, you have no love for it
unless use and exchange are united.
Ring-fence your own greed rather than sanction
the feudal games of your chums. Wet languor
will never destroy this fiscal Hydra.
Unless the jargon be untaught, virtue
cannot 'come to the table': the third way
is prudence, and only virtue leads us
from the country of the blind, etc.
The man who walks away from his bonus
without remorse is no toga-party
emperor amazed by plastic laurels.

XXII

Children of the Manse grouped around the throne
like dear ornaments, beware internal
revolt and hatred. In the olden days
the disjecta membra of false prophets
(square-deal scurf, the pint that thinks it's a quart)
soon left you feeling yourself again. Time-
less products with universal appeal.
Today our customers know no better
yet it's harder to make cheap cuts look like
meaty diadems, and the market in
thrush cream and stool softener tends to queer
the mnemonic pitch. Breaking into song
at least once a day keeps the crunch and snap
of Anglo-Saxon from falling idle.

XXIII
On the matter of hardened defenses

Foreign muck washes in on the tide, boxes
faded and bitten, spat fruit, drained ampoules,
motherboard shards and Barbie-doll torsos
fizzing detergent. This sea-garden clangs
its phantom bells. Eryngium and horned
poppies are a nice touch, resembling
the crown and crowfoot on spigot mortar
emplacements, but do they really help us
with the issue of disjoined waste? Before
us lie dumb redoubts, bare affines like the
marine decay we could begin to love
if only the spin-out was granular
and could be made to depend on a thing
in which it can not discover itself.

XXIV

When we learn how to preserve the future,
the notion of it, beyond the swap-rates
and the divine realm where values never
decline, there might be time enough to stay
out on the marsh at dusk without numpty
longing or the need for fiduciary
tokens and see the strange light rising that
some say misleads the weary traveller.
The real world has not yet become a myth:
attachment to our own field of action
transfigured on high definition screens
resolves to screen-off the dead and crippled
affirming the Tote, our boys, prevailing winds,
stock cubes and the richly fruited nation.

XXV

A broad interpretation of the facts
issues from a Voice beyond his calling,
some force like an unwritten law claiming
global reach, but strangely localized like
a bath plug or bog roll. Do not disturb
me now, for legal reasons which cannot
be known I am unable to respond
to individual cases like my own.
Merely a proud vassal of the state, who
will see the name engraved on stone, or feel
this dark night of the soul going forward
dropped into an isolated unit?
Heart of flint, it all starts up to the eye
as if it had never happened. End of.

```
Two Gordon Brown Sonnets


Two Gordin Brown Sonnets
Two Golden Brown Sonnets
Twa Garden Brown Sonnets
Twa Gardon Brawn Sonnets
Twat Goldarn Bron Sonnets
Twat Guldan Broon Sonnets
twaf Guardon Broan Sonnets
twaf Gridiron Broth Sonets
raf Guillemot Brod Sonets
rap Guild on Brot sonnets
rapid one Guilt Bronnets
rabid Ron Gelid Bonnets
rab wo on Guiting Punnets
o Rabble Grating Puppet
```

Dear G., left the machine on spin and came away

Notes to
'The Gordon Brown Sonnets'

III

Farley's rusk. Originally made up from stale bread, rusk is now produced from yeast-free wheaten particles. It is used primarily as a binding agent in the refashioning of animal parts as sausages. Since the 1880s a dry biscuit form, trademarked as Farley's Rusks, has been a common constituent of the infant diet, taken as a handy disc for nibbling or mashed in milk. The Rusk enjoys a cultic status among university students. In 1994, Farley's was bought out by Heinz, who, thoughtfully binding heritage with the need for consolidation, renamed the product 'Heinz Farley's Rusks'. In 2006, many of these Rusks were withdrawn by the company due to the incorporation of the weedkiller chlorpropham in their manufacture. The work of the poet Paul Farley, possibly named after the famous juvenile product, frequently takes as an objective correlative the gradual maceration of the rusk in its lactic descent. "I feel a rusk pass / through me, tip to tail, like the express / heading north." 29% sugar.

Fray Bentos. Not to be confused in origin with Imperial Bento, a Chinese restaurant at Thorney Atoll, an outpost lying between Peterborough and Wisbech, Fraille Bento was a Uruguayan monk who dwelt speechlessly and heatlessly in a hovel called 'Snails'. His name was given to his locale, a charcoal-burners' paradise (*del monte*) beside a deep and broad river, which carried vessels of all shapes and sizes. In 1862, Fray Bentos was transformed by the arrival of the German company Liebig, which set up a meat-processing plant. Uruguay "had a lot of beef on the hoof out on the pampa", and Liebig's patented extraction process cleaned up. The Liebig Extract of Meat Company came into being in 1865; following the success of products such as the Oxo cube, it was bought out by meat-packing magnate Sir Edmund Vestey in the late 1920s. Vestey called the Uruguayan factory "El Anglo". Borges' 'Funes the Memorious' is set in Fray Bentos; Ireneo Funes himself is the son of an English doctor at the meat packers. Today, Fray Bentos has recalled a batch of its Minced Beef & Onion Pie (425g) due to pieces of metal being found in the product. The batch had been available at participating Iceland stores. Evocative images of the old Fray Bentos plant can be seen in *World of Interiors*, November 2006, 116-21. The sonnet has minor resonances with Kelvin Corcoran's 'Clearing Out the Household Rubbish' in *TCL* (Durham: Pig Press, 1989).

enthymeme. 'In an enthymeme, the speaker builds an argument with one element removed, leading listeners to fill in the missing piece. On May 1, speaking from the deck of the *USS Abraham Lincoln*, President Bush said, "The battle of Iraq is one victory in a war on terror that began on September the 11th, 2001, and still goes on.... With those attacks, the terrorists and their supporters declared war on the United States. And war is what they got." This is classic enthymematic argumentation: We were attacked on Sept. 11, so we went to war against Iraq. The missing piece of the argument— "Saddam was involved in 9/11"—didn't have to be said aloud for those listening to assimilate its message.' (Paul Waldman, *Washington Post*, September 2003.) 'One of the Soviet Georgia's senior citizens thought Dannon was an excellent yogurt. She ought to know. She's been eating yogurt for 137 years.' (Dannon TV advert, 1970s.)

IV
The archaeology of the tinned pie, as recounted by Timothy Brittain-Catlin in 'Stock in Trade', *World of Interiors*, November 2006: 'And the hulk of the El-Anglo works looms in the background like a persistent admonishment...'

V
Cf. James Hurdis, *The Favourite Village* (Bishopstone, Sussex: Printed at the author's own press, 1800), passim.

fauces. The isthmus of the fauces.

VI
Scheurich vase. Scheurich Keramik (1954 -), leading producers of the once reviled but now highly prized West German art pottery of the 60s and 70s. Manufacturers of the once-popular device known as the Rumtopf, an earthenware jar designed to pulp down fruit.

wings take dream. A phrase coined by George W. Bush.

VII
Cf. Horace, *Epistles* I.xi.27:
Caelum, non animum mutant qui trans mare currunt.

grebo. The Seaside Grebo were ancient inhabitants of the area now known as Maryland County. Prior to the civilizing force of the

Euro-American colonists, the Grebo daubed themselves with white clay to symbolize a *ku* (spirit), danced to the spirits wearing carved wooden masks, chipped their teeth to sharp points, and spread human blood on their leaders' ankle-rings, which they believed to be animate. In *Themis: A Study of the Origins of Greek Religion* (London: Merlin Press, 1989, 17f.), Jane Harrison ascribes the origin of the Titans to the ritual coming-of-age practices of the *kouretes*, who used gypsum in a similar way to the Grebo. The Titans, she says, were originally men who daubed themselves with white clay (from τιτανος, *gypsum*) in order to perform initiation rites associated with the passage from child- to man-hood. Perhaps this explains how the name grebo became associated in the 1970s with British fairground 'grease-boys', those virile attendants of the chair-o-planes, gallopers, and dodgems. The original Titans had the role of symbolically murdering the *Kouretes*, young men figured as *daimones* or attendants of the gods who invoke Themis and Dike, the spirits of a time before society and religion became differentiated. According to Harrison, this symbolic death is the basis of the boys' rebirth into the tribe: until each boy has put away his childhood, he cannot become 'socialized, part of the body politic.' The development of a distinctive 'seaside' language is another point of contact. See Gordon Innes, *A Grebo-English Dictionary* (Cambridge: Cambridge University Press, 1967); and Frank Norman, *Dodgem Greaser: Memoirs of a Fairground Boy* (London: Corgi, 1972). The 'greaser' is also a stereotype of the double-crossing Mexican, evinced in early cinematic narratives such as *Tony the Greaser* (1911) and *The Greaser's Revenge* (1914)—cf. the bandits in John Ford's *The Treasure of the Sierra Madre* (1949): 'I don' need no stinking papers!'

VIII

The list of plants in this sonnet is derived from the *trompe-l'oeil* panels of the Faisanderie at Chantilly.

IX

Tony Lopez. British poet and Professor in Poetry, much influenced by U.S. writers associated with the programmatic yet apparently ineffable Language movement. *Data Shadow* is a sequence of fifty sonnets published by Reality Street Editions in the Millennial year.

X

Cambridge. The origin of this city is not precisely known, save that the Romans considered it the farthest practicable point in the fens where they could take transport from the Midlands. 'Further N,' says Pevsner (1954), 'the fens made communications impossible.' An Anglo-Saxon community sprang up after the fifth-century, known as Grantchester and then Grantbridge. Little remains of the medieval commercial town in existence prior to the arrival of the *Studium Generale*; fragments of the Leper Hospital and Milne Street are notable exceptions. Shrouded in darkness also are the thirteenth-century origins of the *Studium*, except that there were migrations from the University of Oxford (itself geographically mistaken for Stamford) at the end of the twelfth century and from Paris in the thirteenth. 'Such migrations testify to unrest and usually to riots.' Cambridge today presents a magnificent façade, its colleges factured from inferior clunch-faced clunch rubble and brick, its stately gardens and riverine walkways leading out to a series of concentric suburban rings clearly modelled on the plan of the universe in *The Divine Comedy*. Since the 1960s, the city has been the centre of a dazzling array of poetic talent.

orators. Cf. Chapter 1 of Hegel's shorter *Logic* (1830).

Cf. the Charlie Parker Sextet, 'Drifting on a Reed' and 'Bongo Beep' (1947), and *Lycidas*, 123-4: 'And when they list, their lean and flashy songs / Grate on their scrannel-pipes of wretched straw'. Milton is clearly thinking of Virgil's line 'stridenti miserum stipula disperdere carmen' (*Eclogues*, III.27). When, in his 1927 Loeb edition of Virgil, H. Rushton Fairclough has Menalcas ask 'Was it not you, Master Dunce, who at the cross-roads used to murder a sorry tune on a scrannel straw', he uses Milton's nonce-word 'scrannel' for *stridenti*.

bollocks. Cf. John Wycliffe, *Bible* (1382), Leviticus xxii, 24: "Al beeste, that... kit and taken a wey the ballokes is, ye shulen not offre to the Lord..." The later version has 'priuy membris', reminding us of privy council, etc. "A high official with the Gilbertian title of Lord West of Spithead... a security advisor to Gordon Brown, was referring to Tony Blair's assertion that invading countries and killing innocent people did not increase the threat of terrorism at home. 'That was clearly bollocks,' said his lordship, who warned of a perceived 'linkage between the US, Israel and the UK' in the horrors inflicted on Gaza and the effect on the recruitment of terrorists in Britain." Lord Spithead should have realized that Blair was obliged to deceive the demos because he had a higher objective in mind: the systematic negation of naturalized spirit. As Hegel states in the *Phenomenology*, "War is the spirit and form in which the essential moment of ethical substance, the absolute freedom of ethical self-consciousness from all and every kind of existence, is manifestly confirmed and realized." (Trans. J. B. Baillie. 2nd edn, revised. London: George Allen and Unwin, 1949, 497.) The Labour government's massive overemphasis on the family and penates appears to the general observer as a typically weak attempt to rescue the Thatcherite mantra of "only individuals and families" for a post-welfare liberal consensus based on incitement to reproduction. The nuclear household not only locks the populace into a cosy necessity that has its members pinging endlessly from estate-agency to right-or wrong-school to supermarket sweep, but entails the simple logic of increase: more repro means more votes. Dialectically, however, the point is to nurture the conditions under which martial craving equals universal self-consciousness. The more youth and young manhood becomes suffocated by privatized family values, the more it seeks to negate what it experiences as mere 'ornamentation' into idealized extremity. "The negative side of the community, suppressing the isolation of individuals within its own bounds, but originating activity directed beyond those bounds, finds the weapons of its warfare in individuals." (idem.)

Browne, in the *Pseudoxia*, writes of how the citizens of Rome were never suffered to know the correct name of their city, "lest the name thereof being discovered unto their enemies, their Penates and Patronal God might be called forth by charms and incantations." (*The Works of Sir Thomas Browne*. ed. Charles Sayre. Vol. I. Edinburgh: John Grant, 1912, 139-40.) Politicians typically withhold truths from common people, revealing their 'visible design' but concealing the 'capital intention'; in doing so, they end up deceiving themselves, "and continually deluded by others, they must needs be stuffed with Errors, and even over-run with these inferiour falsities; whereunto whosoever shall resign their reasons, either from the Root of deceit in themselves, or inability to resist such trivial deceptions from others, although their conditions and fortunes may place them many Spheres above the multitude; yet they are still within the line of Vulgarity, and Democratical enemies of truth."

XI

Brownian noise. Results show that noise inlet spectra can be classified into two categories, pseudo-Brownian resonant noise and white or pink Large band noise, depending on the spectral density distribution. See also "random walk" in sonnet XVII.

Eyes here. Cf. 'The Sand-Man' of E.T.A. Hoffman's *Nachtstücken.* Freud, in 'Das Unheimliche' (1919), ignores the bulk of this story in his desire to focus on the implications of the 'Eyes here! Eyes here!' passage for his theory of the castration complex. Little Nathaniel, driven to distraction by Coppelius / Coppola's castrating gaze, runs about shrieking the words of Johnny Cash's 'Ring of Fire'. The eye and the ring are two of Paul Celan's nodal terms; in *Atemwende,* the poem beginning "Erblinde schon heute: / auch die ewigkeit steht voller Augen" ("Go blind at once, today: / eternity too is full of eyes") is followed by one beginning "Engholztag unter / netznervigem Himmelblatt" ("Ring narrowing Day under / the heavenleaf's web of veins"). The translations here are from Nikolai Popov and Heather McHugh's *glottal stop: 101 poems by paul celan* (Hanover: Wesleyan University Press, 2000). The significance of "101" poems escapes me—except that there is an odd popular publishing trend for anthologies based on this number: *101 Poems to Force you to Fall in Love; 101 Poems by Prize-winning Pests; 101 Poems to put in Room 101,* and suchlike. As for "glottal stop", there may be an uncanny correspondence between the castration complex and Blair and Brown's woebegotten attempts to ingratiate themselves with the "ordinary people" (estuarine delivery, shirt sleeves, joker smiles), but I don't know what it is. Cf. Sonnet I, 13-14 above.

XII

Step away from the pie. I thought I'd made this up, but it seems to have its origin in the amusing NBC situation comedy *Wings* (1990).

ash stranger. Cf. Coleridge, 'Frost at Midnight', 23-5:

> How oft, at school, with most believing mind,
> Presageful, have I gazed upon the bars,
> To watch that fluttering *stranger*!

XIII

plum. Cf. various works by William Carlos Williams, Pound's discussion of the origins of 'In a Station of the Metro' in *Gaudier-Brzeska* (1916), and 'Tabito's Plum-blossom Party', in Edwin A. Cranston, ed. and trans., *A Waka Anthology. Volume One: The Gem-glistening Cup* (Stanford University Press, 1993), 536-50.

Noah. Cf. Genesis, 6-9.

Cf. Horace, *Epistles*, I. xviii:

> quid de quoque viro et cui dicas, saepe videto.
> percontatorem fugito: nam garrulus idem est,
> nec retinent patulae commissa fideliter aures,
> et semel emissum volat irrevocabile verbum.
> non ancilla tuum iecur ulceret ulla puerve
> intra marmoreum venerandi limen amici,
> ne dominus pueri pulchri caraeve puellae
> munere to parvo beet aut incommodus angat.
> qualem commendes etiam atque etiam aspice, ne mox
> incutiant aliena tibi peccata pudorem.
> fallimur et quondam non dignum tradimus: ergo
> quem sua culpa premet, deceptus omitte tueri,
> ut penitus notum, si temptent crimina, serves
> tuterisque tuo fidentem praesidio: qui
> dente Theonino cum circumroditur, ecquid
> ad te post paulo ventura pericula sentis?
> nam tua res agitur, paries cum proximus ardet,
> et neclecta solent incendia sumere vires.

XIV

Nick Drake. 1960s/70s troubadour, known for his superb guitar technique and poignant melancholy songs, now commandeered by Vicks to help smooth away hacking coughs and nasal congestion.

Black Shuck. Hellhound of East Anglian legend. The beast is said to haunt the vast shores of north Norfolk, particularly the zone between Sheringham and Overstrand. In 1577, Shuck (or Shock) terrorised the inhabitants of Bungay and Blythburgh in Suffolk, and has occasionally made it over to the fenland city of Cambridge. Cf. Nick Drake's 'Black Dog'.

XV

Alec Guinness. Cf. *The Man in the White Suit,* dir. Alexander Mackendrick (Ealing Studios, 1951).

hath no man a home. Ezra Pound, *Canto* XLV: the quotation should read 'With usura hath no man a house of good stone', but since possibly 1979, and certainly since 1997, 'home' has displaced the word 'house' for domicile, just as 'family' has overcome 'individual', 'group', and any body eligible for care. Instead of 'common', 'working', or 'lower', they now say 'ordinary'.

riding westward. Cf. Donne, 'Goodfriday, 1613. Riding Westward': 'Hence is't, that I am carryed towards the West / This day, when my Soules forme bends toward the East.' A recent trend in romantic scholarship speculates that Wordsworth's 'Stepping Westward' (1807) presages an interest in the new horizon of America; yet it is more likely an allusion to Donne's eschatology, shorn of its dialectic: 'And stepping westward seemed to be / a kind of *heavenly* destiny.'

XIX

the crown of horny rays. Gerard Manley Hopkins, *Journal,* Sept. 24th, 1870.

holy light. Cf. Benvenuto Cellini, *Autobiography.* Trans. John Addington Symonds (New York: Modern Library, 1927), 273-4.

XX

Argos. What are the origins of this shopping precinct- and catalogue-based perennial? *Argus panoptes* immediately springs to mind. But in fact this trade empire is named after the rebranding of Green Shield Stamps that took place in 1972 following the director's holiday in the Greek city of Argos. From a Cultural Studies perspective, this means that Peter Gabriel's mirthless pun "knights of the Green Shield Stamp and shout", from the 1973 album *Selling England by the Pound,* was already tinged with nostalgia. Cf. J.H. Prynne, *News of Warring Clans* (London: Trigram, 1977): "You stamp about / looking for more cheap cuts and square deals." It is puzzling, though not beyond all conjecture, why people consider this poet so *difficult.* What could be plainer than

Good
taste was shunted into the slogan vestry and
reconstructed as billboard nostalgia: the purest
central dogma in the history of trash.

what more accessible than

> if you're not the cash
> you must be the food, yer dumb git.

Surely Simon Armitage in all his glory was never arrayed as one of
these.

XXI

toga-party / emperor. Cf. Horace, *Odes*, II. ii and x.: "regnum et
diadema tutum / deferens uni propriamque laurum": "*proprius* is
much stronger than *suus* and expresses that which is a permanent
possession and not merely hired, borrowed, or held for a season."
(*Opera*, with notes by Thomas Ethelbert Page, Arthur Palmer, and
A. S. Wilkins. London: Macmillan, 1910, 245.)
Also Andrew Marvell, 'The Garden', 1-2.

In 2009, ministers complained that the global economy was in
meltdown, which effectively absolved them from any sense of
culpability. You just had to keep saying the word "global" and
everything would be all right. In truth, the crash was a carefully
unplanned strategy to secure top-end capital. Having privatized
public utilities, the next step was to divert tax from the public to
the private realm, insuring corporate businesses against their self-
destruction. The new privatized welfare state put to bed the tired
and divisive notion that if you wanted quality public services you
had to pay for them. Now, those poor and foolish enough to be
paying tax had to accept that they were being charged increasing
amounts of money for the downkeep of essential provision, with
the funds top-sliced to pay for the upkeep of financial "service"
they were already buying after tax. It was perhaps the most brilliant
version of stand and deliver yet devised.

Bring me your white metal. Some years ago, I received an invitation to a
performance in St. Pancras by a Mr. Aidan Andrew Dun, author of

Vale Royal and Other Poems. A handbill accompanying the invitation card told of alchemical riches beyond compare, all rendered into mellifluous verse by the Poet, who himself outshines popular minstrels, stand-up comedians, and music hall variety acts alike.

XXII

Children of the Manse grouped around the throne. Overheard in the street in Ampney Crucis, Gloucestershire.

thrush… stool. I am put in mind of the song thrush, *Turdus philomelos,* commonly found across Britain and especially fond of the South East and Anglian regions. It is justly celebrated for the "sip-sip-sip" of its bosky warblings and the "tap-tap-tap" of its snail-bashing sessions. Professor Robertson directs me to an academic essay on Hardy's poetry that referred, by typographical error, to 'The Darkling Thrust'.

Why are these "stool softeners" always projected at women? Perhaps because of an underlying fear in corporate men that they will be tripped up by the hard stools they imagine women wield? Elizabeth Barrett Browning saw this perfectly; as she writes in *Aurora Leigh,* 3.II.456-60:

> The works of women are symbolical.
> We sew, sew, prick our fingers, dull our sight,
> Producing what? A pair of slippers, sir,
> To put on when you're weary—or a stool
> To stumble over and vex you… "curse that stool!"

XXIII

crown and crowfoot. Proprietary marks found on hardened defenses.

XXIV

strange light rising. the *ignis fatuus,* otherwise known as the lambent flame, Will-o'-the-Wykes, *feu follet,* spunky, mad crisp, etc. A phosphorescent apparition that hovers or flits over marshes and graveyards, most likely the spontaneous combustion of gases emitted by rotting organic matter. Cf. Hegel, *Phenomenology,* 719: "Just as that wise man of old searched in his own thought for what was worthy and good, but left it to his 'Daimon' to find out and decide the petty contingent content of what he wanted to know—whether it was good for him to keep company with this or that person, or good for one of his friends to go on a journey, and such like unimportant things; in the same way the universal consciousness draws the knowledge about the contingent from birds, or trees, or fermenting earth, the steam from which deprives the self-conscious mind of its sanity of judgement." Cf. H. Rider Haggard, *She* (1886): "Above me, as I lay, shone the eternal stars, and there at my feet the impish marsh-born balls of fire rolled this way and that, vapour-tossed and earth-desiring, and me-thought that in the two I saw a type and image of what man is, and what perchance man may one day be, if the Living Force who ordained him and them should so ordain this also."

XXV

Heart of flint. Cf. Spenser, *The Faerie Queene*, I.ii.26.

Lightning Source UK Ltd.
Milton Keynes UK
UKOW05f2310300813

216291UK00001BA/9/P